CLOUDSHIP

99

A collection of poems

LINEÉ

CLOUDSHIP 99

MILTON & HUGO L.L.C.
4407 Park Ave., Suite 5
Union City, NJ 07087, USA

Website: *www. miltonandhugo.com*
Hotline: *1- 888-778-0033*
Email: *info@miltonandhugo.com*

Ordering Information:
Quantity sales. Special discounts are granted to corporations, associations, and other organizations. For more information on these discounts, please reach out to the publisher using the contact information provided above.

Library of Congress Control Number: 2024906931
ISBN-13:   979-8-89285-035-3   [Paperback Edition]
                  979-8-89285-036-0   [Digital Edition]

Rev. date: 04/03/2024

CONTENTS

Dedication vii

Foreword.. ix

Introduction xi

Author's Thoughts..xiii

Love 1

The Soul Within...11

Social Justice.. 21

Faith 29

Acknowledgements 47

DEDICATION

I dedicate this book to all the little girls, women, and boys who aspire to dream and make those dreams a reality. To the men who love and support them, I thank and love you too!

FOREWORD

by Frank E. Dobson, Jr., PhD

This is the first book of poetry by this particular literary artist. Her poetic voice is quiet and lyrical. Her poems speak of love, faith, family, dreams, and a range of human emotions. One of the lines in a poem in this collection reads: "If I were to die tomorrow/remember what I stood for." What her poetry "stands for" is strength. There is strength in her words.

She has a strong sense of self. She knows who she is. This poet writes of identity, and she writes poignantly about her identity as a Black woman. She writes of being a Christian, a woman of faith. One of her poems is entitled, "I Honor You." This entire book of poems is one which seeks to honor God. Her poetry is both a pathway and a testimony. Reading this book of poems, your own faith will be strengthened. This is a book of poems that will minister to you, with candor and care. The way in which this writer reveals her heart and soul in this book of poems will show you the depth of her convictions.

Her convictions are to God, family, and humanity. She is a mother, a nurturer, with a warrior spirit. She cares about social justice issues and the plight of the marginalized. Her words take the reader on a spiritual journey, aboard "Cloudship 99," which is an apt metaphor for this book of poems. This book will touch your spirit. It will abide with you.

This book of poetry will do you good. It is a gift to humanity. Read it. Find your favorites. Read them over and over again. Share these poems with loved ones and friends. Let us thank this poet for her courage and her deep love. Let us treasure these poems, and congratulate this poet for her artistry within this, her first book of poems. Let us hope she continues on her poetic journey, aboard "Cloudship 99," sharing her wisdom, insights, and gifts with the world.

INTRODUCTION

"Never cease praying and giving thanks, God is so great!" Lineé

As a little girl, I watched my grandmother get on her hands and knees and pray. Like her mother, my mommy has prayed for and over me. I, as a mother, pray for and over my daughter and her family. I was raised in church, where my grandmother was head of the nursery, so watching my grandmother lovingly care for and nurture other children was one of many ways in which she displayed love. Much of her life and her love for Christ was shown in how my granny cared for others. I am in awe by God's selfless LOVE although we are flawed. I only pray that I am a living example in my walk and talk. I am far from perfect, but I want to live like my grandmother lived and love as she did so those who cross my path can experience my love for them.

AUTHOR'S THOUGHTS

"There is no time stamp on life's opportunities. We limit ourselves when we limit our minds." Lineé

The very thing we find ourselves running from is often the very thing the Holy Spirit leads us to. To hear the words, "we need you" "our little girls need you" so they have someone who looks like them to aspire to. Such weighted words, but with those words comes an assignment. The assignment to be better for our future generations is in our capable hands when God leads. I always ask HIM what he wants from me, but it is not about what HE wants from me, but more importantly what HE wants for them. A glimmer of hope in what appears to be a dark world, a light at the end of a tunnel or the pot of gold at the end of a rainbow. He wants our children to experience unlimited opportunities, but most of all HE wants them to be and feel loved, cherished, and cared for. HE wants HIS children to dream BIG and know they can do anything their hearts' desire and that includes me.

"I want to be your last, best everything." Lineé

LOVE

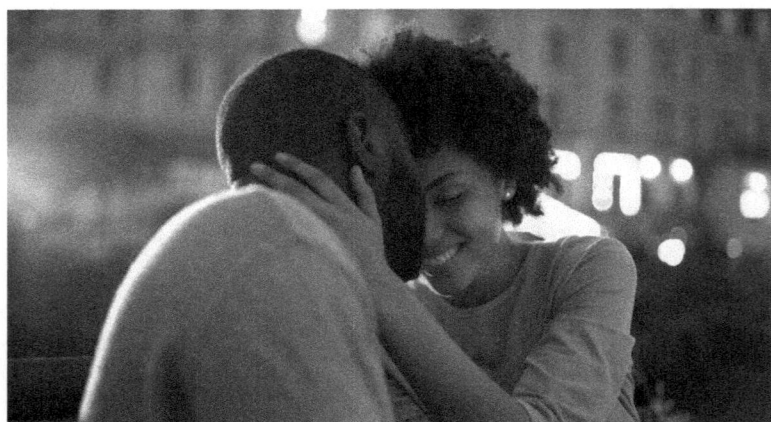

Will you love me?

To love me is to love
My offspring and her offspring
Before me and all my family between me

To love me is to
Show me tenderness
In the wilderness
When my mind is on some kind of craziness
Because it won't always be happiness

To love me is to love me through my weakness and
sickness
Because as this body ages, there may be all kinds of
brokenness

After all, to have me and to hold me will be on another
level of loving me

Compass

Will you be my compass?
Guide me through life's unchartered territories
The highs and lows of the peaks and valleys of this
mountainous terrain
Explore the North to my mind and stimulate me with
mental gasms

Will you hold my hand?
As we experience our first and last bests of everything
together
While traveling south to my heart, your hidden
treasure
Be careful because this heart is fragile

Will you embrace me?
As your arms stretch wide from east to west and we
meet somewhere in the middle
Engulf me with the essence of your presence
And I will promise to stand by your side
Until the end of our time
As long as you will be my compass

Kind of Love

I'm yearning for that
Greet you at the front door
Kind of love

That holding hands
Opening the car door
Chivalry isn't dead
Kind of love

The mere thought of you
Has me weak in the knees
Kind of love

The sound of your voice
Your whispers of sweet nothings
As you nibble on my ear
Makes my heart turn somersaults
Kind of love

A communication only you and I understand, as you gather me
in your arms
The taste of your sweet lips on mine
Kind of love

Is this KIND OF LOVE just an illusion?
A fleeting fantasy or emotional imagery of words
OFTEN left unspoken kind of love?

Love Is a Verb

Love is a verb, an action word, not a warm, cozy feeling
It's warm, blue skies, butterflies and the beauty of the trees
that were created especially for me
It's the air that I breathe because HE breathed life into me
It's the honey do list, the soft caress, and the tenderness
The just because flowers that remove the showers of tears
It's not broken promises
Or a crushed heart
Or abandoned feelings left void
Love is a verb, an action word

Love Loss

Life and living are not promised
Cherish the seconds, minutes, hours and days with the ones
you love and who genuinely love you
To have loved in your lifetime and to have lost your lifetime love
is undeniably the greatest loss
 You don't know me, but I knew of someone you loved and pray
for your strength in the coming days and beyond
It doesn't get easier, so don't allow anyone to put a timetable on
your grieving process
Hold and hug your children tighter, love on them longer and
love yourself through
Lean on God and hold onto HIS words and promises
HE will carry you through

Do You Know Me?

If I were to die tomorrow
Could you say you knew all the intimate pieces of me?
The ones I treasure
My purest parts and my deepest thoughts
Those things that cannot be measured

If I were to die tomorrow
Would you remember me as I was?
Or the beautiful flower I blossomed into
Where every leaf and petal told a different story
Of my love, my life and its glory

If I were to die tomorrow
Remember what I stood for
As every layer unfolds
The key to my heart is now told
In its rawest form

"I've been quiet for so long I feel as though I have finally found my voice." Lineé

THE SOUL WITHIN

The Me You See

Rose filtered glasses
Covered the pain of my tears
Designer brands covered my heart in part, but
I am not the me you see

Meaningless relationships from my past
2013 and 2001 to be exact, were masks
My Halloween costumes in disguise
Because
I am not the me you see

Heart shattered and broken
Tear stained pillows
Dreams deferred
I put up a good façade STILL
I am not the me you see

Peace in Pieces

The perfect imperfection
The bastard child
I merely exist
As a reminder of the sole transgression
The little secret, should she keep it?

Scolded harshly
Treated differently
She is her vanilla and he is her chocolate
Her drug of choice, the prodigal son
The forbidden fruit or the delectable dessert
Which one does she treasure?

Whispered about, shunned away
A constant reminder of that very day remains
A heart shattered into many pieces
Left alone until the beat of her heart ceases
Will she ever find her peace amongst the pieces where she
finally belongs?

Finding Me

In 2023, I discovered ME

I learned

I have a voice

I have a gift

I have a heart

And I FOUND LOVE

      A greater love for life

      A love and appreciation for beauty

      A love for passion

      A love for intimacy

      A love for romance

With all this love, the most important thing is, I found a love for ME

Beauty in Me

The complexion of my skin doesn't define the person
within
Flaws and all, there is beauty I see
When the mirror stares back at me
Tired eyes,
Thundered thighs,
Batwings, and
Saggy breasts
All tell my story of how God
So distinctly made me in HIS image
And NOW I am beautifully, fearfully and wonderfully
made WHOLE

Authenticity

I shouldn't have to code switch
For my very existence
In a world where my very Blackness
Causes fear amongst racists
Where the skin I am in is poppin' with melanin
And my confidence
Exudes in my walk, my talk and my stance

My spoken word is eloquently conveyed
Through the rhythm and rhymes I've made
I am capable of articulating
Without changing my dialect
So, they feel threatened
By my intellect

Plight of a Black Woman

Some women will GET IT, while others choose not to
Some will continue to walk with blinders on because
they don't walk in my shoes or our shoes
After all, they don't have to!
To be called an offensive word, to be told I am less than
when I am just as educated and, in some cases, more
than
To find ways to keep my child, my grandchildren, and
my family safe so they are not threatened or killed
because their skin is of a different shade
To safely carry a child to term and know that my
physician will care for me because it is morally and
ethically the right thing to do
Tears because of my fears, not because of fragility!

NO !

NO - a simple sentence that stands alone

NO - uncomplicated to some, but difficult for others to comprehend

NO - the word I am more comfortable boldly speaking now

I gave to those who used me and never got it back

I can now find peace in my NO and you're never getting it back!

"I must take a stand for social justice!
If I am still and I remain silent, then I am allowing
oppressors to win this fight." Lineé

SOCIAL JUSTICE

A Cry for Help

Today I cried
For the little boy who's lost his soul inside
Lost to a life on the streets
Where crystal meth and other homeless victims of
America's poverty are his peeps
We talked about God during our encounter
He shared with me his belief in a Higher Power
We bonded on hip hop and rap
While I carefully listened and learned that methadone
clinics are a trap
To keep the vicious circle of dependency on loop
We fail United States citizens, our families and our
troops
Will we ever get back to humanity?
When we begin loving on friends and family without
boundaries
Love sees no color, he or she or they could be your
brother, father, sister or mother

Toxic Elixir

One sip, two sip, three sip, POUR
That liquid poison down your throat once more
The one your body always craves FOR
Five clink, six
Ice cubes hit the glass and the juice for that toxic mix
As you intoxicate your body for that quick fix
Seven, eight, nine and ten
Your disillusion to the danger drinking poses within
High end Whiskey, Gin, and Cog(nac)
Compared to the Mad-Dog 2020, Paul Mason and E&J
throwbacks
Tip the bottles 'til they're empty again!
The vicious cycle of your drunken stupor and libations never
ends

Does Humanity Live Here?

How selfish are we or me?
When we can't lead with compassion or empathy
For our fellow man or woman
Have we lost the HUMAN in humanity?

Despite the borders
Love transcends all races and colors
Politics have become made up constructs
Where the men behind it are corrupt
While organized religion and its demons create a world
of division
The world we live in is complete insanity

Wars of Injustice

My eyes are open wide
To the traumas and casualties of genocide
Where women, men and children are used as human shields
For cowardice men and where weapons of mass destruction
yield
Where wrongful convictions negatively affect Black men's lives
Disproportionate sentences to proportionate crimes
The injustices of our justice system threaten the lives of us all
When will we finally take a stand, where each of us is for all of
us hand in hand

"My past doesn't define me because God has redeemed me." Lineé

FAITH

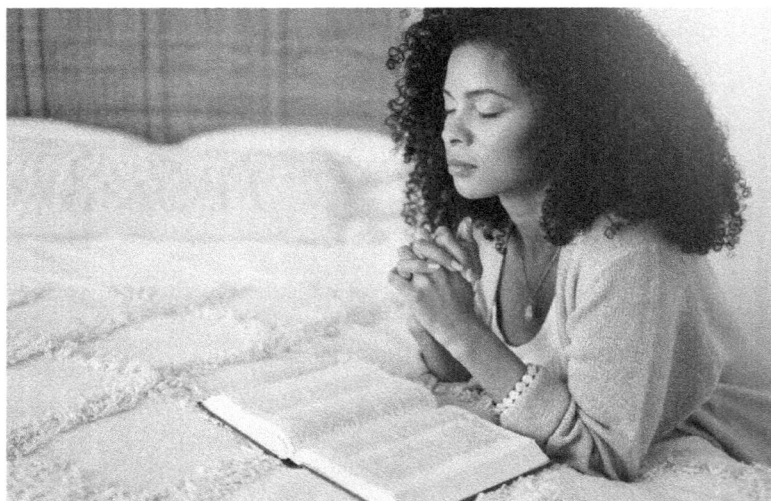

Reflection of YOU

Forever loves are now a memory
In my bitterness I became better
My heart bled for the loves I lost, but
Are my thoughts and actions a reflection of you?

My tongue was a powerful sword
My eyes were the depths to my soul
My stance was rigid, but
My thoughts and actions were NOT a reflection of you

Grace, you gave me
Your mercy saved me
Your perfect love embraced me
NOW my thoughts and actions ARE a reflection of you

Awaken Me

Awaken my spirit oh Lord!
Rescue me from my troubles
For you see all that is within
And breathe new life in me

Awaken my spirit oh Lord!
Protect and guide me!
When the path I see is unclear
In my heart and mind, I know you are near
Your hedge of protection surrounds me

Awaken my spirit oh Lord!
When the devil feels like a stronghold
Let your steadfast love envelope me
Allow me to hear you oh Lord!
For your mighty power and voice comfort me

My Prayer

Lord, I submit to you
Though the trials of life and waiting might be difficult
My patience and strength come from you

When the answers don't come quickly
I know to look for you
To seek you
My comforter, my Rock, my Redeemer
Knowing YOU will see me through
Lord, I thank you!

Pray & Rejoice

In the meantime
In between time
The time is NOW

Wait on the Lord
He hears your cries, but
In the meantime
PRAY

Call upon HIS name
Spread the good news
In between time
REJOICE

Study HIS Word
Follow HIS commandments
Lean not into your own understanding
But remain faithful
The time is NOW!

I HONOR YOU

I honor God with my worship by loving the woman HE created
in me and the women we are meant to be
From the crowns of our heads to the soles of our feet, we are
wonderfully and beautifully made
To think otherwise would be displeasing to God because we are
made in HIS image
Who are we to question or doubt HIS creations?

I honor God with my voice by spreading HIS good news
News that flows through as beautiful melodies in the words I
pen because of HIM
I honor God with my character by willfully giving to HIM and
spending time in the Word
Loving people where they are so they can see HIM in me
Lord, I honor YOU!

Artistry in HIS Tapestry

A resounding I AM HIS permeates through me! I yield to HIS ways knowing if I stay focused on Him and His Word, my paths will no longer be crooked. There is a transformation I have experienced during this season - a renewal of sorts. In my youth, I was quick witted, easy to anger and emboldened to lash out, but God. In this season of life, I have learned to love people more and the importance of forgiveness, grace, and mercy. Today, I stopped to acknowledge the beauty found as I marveled in His wonders. I am enamored by God's love for ALL OF US in the beautiful tapestries HE created. The skies were the most beautiful shades of blue and the trees' greenery sprinkled with colors of lavender and white were perfectly blended. It is in these solo journeys, I marvel in the beauty and reflect on and acknowledge HIM for all HE is doing in and through me.

I'm Sorry

The Love of God and the fear of people and the lack of
humanity motivates me to love on others more and focus
less on my personal woes. Knowing God can prick my heart at
any time, my "act right" must always remain in check. God's
patience, love and kindness gives us cause to pause before
acting or speaking without thought. Because of this, I see me
differently. I see you differently. I see WE differently! For every
unkind word I have said or that "not so nice glare", I apologize.
Let the words I speak always be sweet and kind and reflect the
love, grace and mercy God has shown me.

I AM HIS

I am an underdog in the eyes of many just because there is melanin in my skin, but that melanin does not change the character or the person within

When others rise against me, I must stand strong and firm in my faith and trust in God because to put that same faith and trust in man will disappoint me

My mind and heart are often conflicted because of the evil that surrounds me

I react because my heart has been shattered in pieces as I hear about those who look like me being broken and diminished as though their lives meant nothing and their mere existence is an inconvenience to a society riddled with fools

I must remember I am not the judge nor am I the jury, but I AM HIS

I Failed HIM

When I didn't go to HIM in prayer
When I didn't study HIS Word
When I didn't patiently wait for HIS response
HE didn't fail me, I failed HIM!

When I was unkind to my sisters and brothers
When I spoke and my words hurt
When I doubted
He didn't fail me, I failed HIM

I failed to be slow to anger
I failed to act in love
I failed to be kinder and gentler
I failed HIM, AGAIN!

Alive

No one would get to me quick enough, and the suffering would not be long
I placed my trust in Jesus, in HIM is where my faith belonged
To inflate my lung was a miracle only the hands of the Lord could perform
I am a living testament of HIS greatness and have forever been transformed

The prayers I placed before HIM and the silent tears I cried
I am sure HE heard me because on that day I died
Today, I can boldly say, my faith will not waver
Because during the worst of times and even the best of times, God has given me favor

It was almost 10 years before I shared the story of what happened that day
I am so grateful to God that HE allowed me to stay
I no longer take life for granted now that my feet are firmly planted

I will continue to pray and follow HIS ways
So I might be the light to those who might be experiencing darker days

Forgiveness with God's Promises

In my quiet time, I think, I write, and I pray

I think about my past, past loves and past losses, but not of the humankind

I used to think about regrets, but I don't see them as regrets anymore

They were minor setbacks in the grand scheme of this thing called life

Forgive yourself for those you have hurt, but more importantly forgive those who have hurt you

Your regrets are merely a diversion from the path God has for you

They are a lesson so you can see God's blessings

He promises never to leave his followers, nor to forsake them

and I am holding onto HIS Word because it comforts and consoles us, and then make US WHOLE again

Are You Listening Lord?

In my distress, do you hear me?
When I am weak and broken, can you heal me and make me whole?
When the pains of life hurt or scare me, will you protect me?
When troubles are too much and the path is curved, will you guide me?

Lord, I come humbly before you to sing your praises
Through it all, you uplift and build me
You carry me when I have nothing left in me and my burdens consume me
Though my doubts and fears weigh heavily upon me
I will seek you first in all things – for direction, your protection and comfort
Will you answer?
Lord, I know you are near and hear me

Cloudship 99

The forecast is clear
Sunny skies and puffy white clouds are ahead
You're about to board Cloudship 99
I am your co-pilot Jesus
Sitting at the helm is God

Kindly take your seats and fasten your seatbelts
The angels are here to assist you
The exit rows are in the middle, to the rear and of course near
the pilots' cabin

There may be turbulence
But it's merely the trials and tribulations of life
A slight detour, but you'll reach your destination on time and
safely

Pray and never cease, your pilots answer prayers
Angels surround and protect you
Aboard Cloudship 99

Fear not, on this journey we have you covered and protected
You're anchored in the Lord and Cloudship 99 is preparing for
takeoff

Safe travels!

I hope you have enjoyed my personal reflections, interwoven with the lives of the people I have encountered, on my journey aboard Cloudship 99.

ACKNOWLEDGEMENTS

I would like to praise and honor God for those gentle awakenings at 4:30 AM to complete my Bible studies and for the ability to pen. I would like to thank my life-love and my love-life partner for your unwavering support and encouragement along this journey. To my sister-friends for your constructive criticism and feedback, where would I be without you? Finally, the love of my life, my daughter, I love you beyond infinity and my life became more meaningful the day God blessed me with you.